# THE CHRISTMAS TABLE

THE BEST FROM GONDOLEN'S CHRISTMAS TABLE

# THE CHRIST MAS TABLE

THE BEST FROM GONDOLEN'S CHRISTMAS TABLE

ERIK LALLERSTEDT & MAGNUS LEIDSTEDT
PHOTOS: BRUNO EHRS

ICA BOKFÖRLAG

The secret behind preparing for Christmas, especially the Christmas menu, is to avoid stress, or at least to find time to do all the preparations by working with the clock rather than against it. Being stressed is counter-productive. It is the most effective way to lose time and should be avoided if possible.

The recipe for not falling into the stress trap is to plan far in advance. You can buy Christmas presents any time of year, or at least you can start in November, instead of doing what I did when I was young, when I bought all my presents on Christmas Eve at NK. Of course it worked, but I lost an evening at home with my family, not to mention the preparations for the Christmas table. Even though a lot was done the day before, it was still very stressful.

A practical way to plan the Christmas menu is to write down what you want to serve your guests and then make a shopping list. That can take anywhere from 20 minutes to an entire evening, depending upon your ambitions, differences of opinion or just glögg-testing! Everything doesn't have to be home-made. There are many good things you can buy ready-made, so if you know someone who is an expert at making a particular dish, place an order and serve that on your table. If someone loves paté but can't cook, then just buy the best quality paté you can. And if your father-in-law can't imagine Christmas without pigs' trotters, just tell him that they are bad for the environment!

What I am really saying is to plan, make lists, delegate tasks and decide what to serve according to wishes, abilities and budget. The most important thing is not that there is so much food or as many dishes as possible. The most meaningful part is that you like what you see and experience, and that you enjoy the meal together with those you love. If you don't allow yourself to be rushed, you will have a better Christmas.

P.S: In this book, you will find a selection of what you can serve for Christmas, plus our instructions for how Christmas buffet guests should approach the table. But we must tell you that the preparations for a traditional commercial Christmas buffet table are planned at least six months in advance, before it is presented by 25 chefs, cold buffet managers and pastry chefs here in our kitchen. D.S.

*Erik Lallerstedt*

1 Herring plays the leading role on your first plate. Matjes herring, mustard herring and everyone's favorite, marinated herring. Baltic herring also should appear on this plate. Try it marinated with juniper or with whitefish caviar or served warm, crayfish-style.

2 Time for a new plate. Fill it with smoked, poached or dill-marinated salmon, smoked eel and Professor Lallerstedt's marinated smoked herring with boiled egg halves topped with whitefish caviar and shrimp.

3 Time to move on. Now there's Christmas ham, veal head cheese, patés, dried reindeer and mutton, and moose and liver sausage. Be sure to try our homemade mustard with the ham.

4 Still hungry? Now the temperature is rising and we are serving Jansson's temptation, meatballs, hot sausages, "dopp i grytan" (bread dipped in the broth from the Christmas ham), pork ribs and lutefisk. Try our omelet with shellfish and salmon and enjoy a toast with your guests.

5 There's always room for dessert! Rice cream, ice chocolate, burnt almonds and fried cookies. Mint kisses, figs, dates and caramels. Stuff yourself with glorious mouthfuls of saffron pancakes and biscotti, dream of a white Christmas and invite everyone back next year!

Merry Christmas from
***Erik Lallerstedt***

## CURRY HERRING

**CURRYSILL**

(6 SERVINGS)

1 small apple
3 cm (1¼ inches) leek
Butter
2 teaspoons curry powder
2 dl (¾ cup) mayonnaise
1 dl (⅓ cup) sour cream
6 fillets marinated herring
*(see basic recipe marinated herring page 15)*

Peel and dice the apple and leek. Sauté in butter until shiny. Add the curry powder and sauté a couple minutes more. Let cool. Stir the curry mixture, mayonnaise and sour cream together. Drain the herring very well in a strainer. Cut into diagonal slices. Stir into the curry mixture, mixing well. Refrigerate for at least 24 hours before serving. Garnish with thin apple wedges.

## WHITEFISH CAVIAR-MARINATED BALTIC HERRING

### LÖJROMSGRAVAD STRÖMMING

(6 SERVINGS)

BRINE
2 dl (1 cup) 6% vinegar
4 dl (2 cups) water
2¼ teaspoons salt

500 g (1¼ pounds) fresh Baltic herring fillets
2 dl (1 cup) mayonnaise
1 dl (½ cup) crème fraiche (or sour cream)
1 dl (½ cup) sour cream
2 tablespoons lemon juice
Salt and white pepper
3 tablespoons whitefish caviar, around 60 g (2 ounces)
Fresh dill

Combine vinegar, water and salt. Remove the skin from the herring fillets and place in the brine. Marinate for 8 hours in the refrigerator.

Mix together mayonnaise, crème fraiche, sour cream and lemon juice. Season with salt and pepper. Carefully stir in half the caviar. Drain the herring well in a sieve. Press carefully to remove as much liquid as possible. Cut into slices, then fold into the sauce. To serve, garnish with the remaining caviar and fresh dill.

## JUNIPER-MARINATED BALTIC HERRING
### ENBÄRSGRAVAD STRÖMMING
(10 SERVINGS)

This recipe serves 10 (more on a Christmas table or buffet). It's a little time-consuming to make, but it is worth it!

BRINE
4 dl (1 2/3 cups) 6% vinegar
8 dl (3 1/3 cups) water
1½ tablespoons (4 teaspoons) salt

1 kg (2 pounds) skinless fresh Baltic herring fillets
3½ dl (1¼ cups) sugar
2 tablespoons (5 teaspoons) salt
60 g (2 ounces) juniper berries, crushed in a mortar
2 bay leaves
3 g (¾ teaspoon) sandel (optional)
6 g (1½ teaspoons) allspice berries, crushed in a mortar
15 g (1½ tablespoons) yellow mustard seeds
1 small leek, sliced
3 red onions, sliced
Plucked dill from 6–8 stalks

Combine vinegar, water and salt. Add the herring and let marinate for 1 hour. Drain, discarding the brine. Combine the dry ingredients and spices. Layer the herring in a glass dish with the spice mixture and the vegetables. Layer the herring, side by side, in a single thin layer. Then sprinkle with vegetables and spice mixture. Add a new layer, but with the herring facing in the other direction (Think 90 degree angle). Finish with spice mixture. Let sit at room temperature for a few hours. Cover with plastic wrap and refrigerate for at least 5 days. This herring should keep for at least one month when refrigerated at +4 C (40 F).

## MARINATED HERRING

**INLAGD SILL**

(BASIC RECIPE 6 SERVINGS)

BRINE

6 dl (2½ cups) water
7 dl (3 cups) sugar
7 dl (3 cups) 6% vinegar
2 red onions, sliced
2 carrots, sliced
1 small leek, sliced
1 teaspoon ground cloves
2 teaspoons ground allspice
4 bay leaves

Place all ingredients in a pot and heat to boiling. Let cool overnight. Strain.

6 salt herring fillets, soaked in cold water with careful rinsing for around 8 hours (or purchase pre-soaked herring fillets
1 carrot, thinly sliced
1 chunk leek, thinly sliced
1 onion, thinly sliced
5 whole cloves
10 allspice berries
4 bay leaves

Layer the herring in a jar with the vegetables and spices. Pour over the brine so that everything is covered. Refrigerate for one week before serving. Cut into diagonal slices before serving.

## MUSTARD HERRING
**SENAPSSILL**
(6 SERVINGS)

6 marinated herring fillets
(*see basic recipe page 15*)
1 tablespoon Colman's mustard powder
2 tablespoons Dijon mustard
2 tablespoons mayonnaise
2 tablespoons sugar
1 tablespoon mustard seeds (preferably half yellow, half brown)
2 teaspoons fresh lime juice

Combine all ingredients (except herring), mixing well. Let rest at room temperature for one hour, then mix again. Drain herring fillets well and cut into diagonal slices. Carefully fold the herring into the sauce. Refrigerate overnight.

## LIME-HORSERADISH HERRING
**LIME- OCH PEPPARROTSSILL**
(6 SERVINGS)

8 marinated herring fillets
(*see basic recipe page 15*)
300 g (10 ounces) cream cheese
Grated zest and juice of 1 lime
3 tablespoons dark beer, such as Falcon Bavarian
1 dl (½ cup) crème fraiche or sour cream
1 dl (½ cup) Greek-style thick yogurt or strained natural yogurt
1 tablespoon grated fresh horseradish
1 tablespoon honey
Salt and pepper

Combine all ingredients (except herring), mixing well. Season with salt and pepper. If the sauce is not "hot" enough, add more horseradish. Drain herring fillets well and cut into diagonal slices. Carefully fold into the sauce. Refrigerate at least overnight before serving.

## QUEEN MARGARETHE'S HERRING
**DROTTNING MARGARETHES SILL**
(6 SERVINGS)

6 large matjes herring fillets
100g (½ cup) red currant jelly
2 tablespoons 6% vinegar
¾ dl (⅓ cup) water
1 dl (½ cup) ketchup
2 tablespoons capers
1 red onion, thinly sliced

Soak the herring in cold water for around 4 hours. Drain well. Melt the jelly with the vinegar and water. Stir in the ketchup. Let cool. Cut the herring into 2 cm (¾ inch) slices and carefully fold into the sauce. Refrigerate for at least 24 hours before serving. Just before serving, garnish with capers and onion.

## PROFESSOR LALLERSTEDT'S MUSTARD-MARINATED SMOKED HERRING

### PROFESSOR LALLERSTEDTS SENAPSMARINERADE BÖCKLING

(6 SERVINGS)

*A recipe from Erik's brother*

4 whole smoked herring or small smoked whitefish
5 tablespoons red wine vinegar
3 ½ tablespoons sugar
1 dl (½ cup) sweet Swedish mustard
1 dl (½ cup) coarse Skåne mustard
3 ½ dl (1 ⅓ cups) vegetable oil

GARNISH
5 cm (2 inches) leek, finely diced
1 small red onion, finely chopped
1 handfull dill stalks, chopped

Remove skin and bones from the fish. Arrange the boneless fish in a deep glass dish. Whisk vinegar and sugar until dissolved. Add the mustards and gradually whisk in the oil in a thin stream. Pour the sauce evenly over the fish. Garnish with stripes of leek, red onion and dill.

## HERRING SALAD

**SILLSALLAD**

(6 SERVINGS)

400 g (14 ounces) potatoes
400 g (14 ounces) marinated herring (*see basic recipe page 15*)
150 g (5 ounces) sour pickles
1 onion
2 teaspoons butter
400 g (14 ounces) pickled beets
1 green apple, diced
Salt and pepper

Boil the potatoes until tender, peel and dice. Drain the herring well. Dice the herring and pickles. Chop the onion and sauté in butter until soft. Let cool. Drain and dice the beets. Peel and dice the apple. Combine all ingredients. Season with salt and pepper. Just before serving, garnish with whipped cream and hard-cooked egg wedges, if desired.

*Being stressed*
*is the most effective way*
*to lose time, and it*
*should be avoided if*
*possible.*

## CLASSIC GRAVLAX (MARINATED SALMON)
### KLASSISK GRAVLAX
(10–12 SERVINGS)

1 boneless salmon fillet, around 2 kg (4 ½ pounds), skin on, pinbones removed
3 ½ dl (1 ½ cups) sugar
1 ½ dl (⅔ cup) salt
15 white peppercorns, coarsely ground
1 small bunch dill, around 50 g (2 ounces)

Trim the fish and remove the pinbones with a tweezers. Leave the skin on. Combine sugar, salt and white pepper. Rub the meaty side of the fish with the sugar-salt mixture. Place in a dish just large enough, meat side down. Let rest at room temperature until the sugar and salt have dissolved. Turn the fish. Cut the dill into 1 cm (½ inch) lengths and sprinkle over the fish. Cover the fish with dill. Cover with plastic wrap and refrigerate. Turn the fish every 8 hours for the first 48 hours, then morning and night. After 4–5 days, the salmon is ready. Cut into thin slices and serve with mustard sauce.

## MUSTARD SAUCE FOR GRAVLAX
### SENAPSSÅS TILL GRAVLAX
(6 SERVINGS)

2 tablespoons sugar
2 tablespoons brown sugar
2½ tablespoons red wine vinegar
1 dl (½ cup) sweet Swedish mustard
2 dl (1 cup) corn oil
1–2 tablespoons chopped dill

Whisk both sugars with the vinegar until frothy. Add the mustard. Whisk in the oil in a thin stream, beating until emulsified. Just before serving, stir the dill into the sauce.

## RHODE ISLAND SAUCE
### RHODE ISLANDSÅS
(6 SERVINGS)

3 dl (1¼ cups) mayonnaise
1 dl (scant ½ cup) chili sauce, preferably Heinz
2 tablespoons sherry
2 tablespoons cognac
1 tablespoon Worcestershire sauce
Pinch Cayenne pepper
3 drops Tabasco sauce
Salt and pepper

Combine all ingredients. Season with salt and pepper. Serve in a bowl.

## COLD-SMOKED SALMON WITH VÄSTERBOTTEN-HORSERADISH MIX

### KALLRÖKT LAX MED VÄSTERBOTTEN/PEPPARROTSRÖRA

(6 SERVINGS)

1 dl (½ cup) coarsely grated Västerbotten or sharp cheddar cheese
1 tablespoon finely grated horseradish
4 tablespoons (¼ cup) mayonnaise
2 tablespoons crème fraiche
Freshly ground white pepper
400 g (12 ounces) thinly sliced cold-smoked salmon

Combine all ingredients except the salmon. Cover and refrigerate, preferably overnight. Remove the brown edge of the salmon that was closest to the skin. Arrange on individual plates and top with a spoonful of the cheese-horseradish mixture. Garnish with dill and chives or red onion, if desired.

### EGG HALVES WITH SHRIMP, ANCHOVIES AND MAYONNAISE
**ÄGGHALVOR MED RÄKOR, ANSJOVIS OCH MAJONNÄS**
(6 SERVINGS)

3 eggs
6 rounds cocktail bread
1 dl (½ cup) hand-shelled shrimp
2 tablespoons mayonnaise
1 tablespoon chopped dill
1 tablespoon lemon juice
Salt and pepper
6 anchovy fillets

Boil the eggs for around 10 minutes. Remember, they should actually simmer, not boil. Peel and halve lengthwise. Cut thin slices off the bottoms so the egg halves stand level. Place on cocktail bread. Combine shrimp, mayonnaise, dill and lemon juice. Season with salt and pepper. Spoon the shrimp mixture onto the egg halves. Top with anchovies.

### PICKLED BEETS
**INLAGDA RÖDBETOR**

1 kg (2¼ pounds) fresh beets
4 cm (1¾ inch) length fresh horseradish
6 cloves
5 allspice berries
5 bay leaves
5 black peppercorns
Herring brine, *see recipe page 15*

Cook the beets in water to cover. Large beets take around 1 hour. Test for tenderness with a skewer. They should "feel like" boiled potatoes. When done, plunge into cold water. Peel. Peel and cut the horseradish into small dice. Place the beets in a lidded jar with the horseradish and seasonings. Pour over brine to cover. Replace the lid. Refrigerate for at least three days before serving.

### VEAL HEAD CHEESE
**KALVSYLTA**
(MAKES 2)

1½ kg (3¼ pounds) veal shoulder, salted
1 large onion
2 carrots
1 chunk celeriac
1 parsnip
10 cloves
10 allspice berries
10 white peppercorns
5 bay leaves
Bouillon powder
Gelatin powder

Be sure to order the meat well in advance.

Place the meat in a pot. Add cold water to cover and heat to boiling. Boil for 5 minutes. Drain and rinse the meat in cold water (to remove any traces of blood and protein, so that the stock will be clear).

Place the meat in a pot. Add water to cover. Heat to boiling, skimming well. Peel the vegetables and cut into chunks. Add to the pot with the seasonings. Cover and let simmer over low heat for at least 5 hours. Remove the meat from the cooking liquid and let cool. Strain and measure the stock. Add 50 g (1 ¾ ounces) bouillon powder and 30 g (2 ounces) gelatin powder for every liter (4 cups) stock. When cool, remove the fat, membrane and gristle from the meat. Separate into coarse shreds. Cut the meat over the fibers. Arrange the meat in two loaf pans. Pour over the stock to cover. Stir with a fork so that all the meat comes into contact with the stock. Cover with plastic wrap and refrigerate overnight. Just before serving, unmold and cut into slices.

### JANSSON'S TEMPTATION
**JANSSONS FRESTELSE**
(6 SERVINGS)

1 kg (2½ pounds) potatoes
1 large onion
4 dl (1⅔ cups) light cream
1 tin anchovies, around 200 g (7 ounces) 20 fillets
Salt and pepper
Butter
Breadcrumbs

Preheat the oven to 175 C (350 F). Peel and coarsely grate the potatoes. Peel and thinly slice the onion. Place onion, potatoes and cream in a heavy saucepan. The liquid should just cover the potatoes. Heat to boiling and add the anchovies. Season with salt and pepper. Pour into a greased ovenproof dish. Bake for around 45 minutes. Remove from the oven and dot with butter and sprinkle with crumbs. Bake for 10 minutes more.

## GRILLED CHRISTMAS HAM
**JULSKINKA MED GRILJERING**

3 egg yolks
2 dl (¾ cup) Erik's Christmas mustard according to the recipe or same amount Swedish mustard
1 cooked ham, any size
1 dl (½ cup) fine breadcrumbs

Preheat the oven to 175 C (350 F). Whisk together egg yolks and mustard. Brush a thin layer over the ham. Sift an even layer of breadcrumbs over the ham. Grill or bake until golden brown.

## ERIK'S CHRISTMAS MUSTARD
**ERIKS JULSENAP**

50 g (¼ cup) brown sugar
½ dl (¼ cup) red wine vinegar
2 tablespoons yellow mustard seeds
2 tablespoons brown mustard seeds
5 dl (2½ cups) Swedish mustard
1½ dl (1½ cups) coarse Skåne mustard
40 g (2¼ ounces) Colman's mustard powder
½ dl (¼ cup) dark sugar or corn syrup
1 dl (½ cup) orange blossom honey
2 tablespoons orange juice concentrate
2 tablespoons cognac
Grated zest of 1 washed orange

Melt the brown sugar in the vinegar. Crush the mustard seeds in a mortar. Combine all ingredients very well. Transfer to jars with lids. Store for a week before serving.

## BROWN CABBAGE
**BRUNKÅL**
(6 SERVINGS)

1 large head cabbage
3 tablespoons butter
1 dl (½ cup) sugar or corn syrup
3 dl (1 ½ cups) chicken stock
1 dl (½ cup) 6% vinegar
1 tablespoon salt
Freshly ground white pepper

Quarter the cabbage and remove the core. Shred as finely as possible. Fry in a large pan in butter until golden brown. Add the syrup and cook for a few more minutes. Add the stock and cook, stirring frequently, until most of the liquid has evaporated. Season with vinegar, salt and pepper.

## CREAMED KALE
**LÅNGKÅL**
(6 SERVINGS)

3 dl (1½ cups) chicken stock
2 packages frozen kale (800 g/1¾ pounds)
1 dl (½ cup) whipping cream
1 dl (½ cup) crème fraiche (or more cream)
Salt and white pepper
1 tablespoon butter
2 tablespoons chopped parsley

Heat the stock to boiling and add the kale. Simmer for 3–4 minutes. In another saucepan, heat the cream and crème fraiche to simmering. Drain the cabbage and fold into the cream. Season with salt and pepper. Just before serving, stir in the butter and parsley.

## PICKLED RED CABBAGE
**RÖDKÅL**
(6 SERVINGS)

1 head red cabbage
1 large or 2 small red onions
3 red winter apples
2 tablespoons butter
1 dl (½ cup) black currant jelly
3 tablespoons concentrated black currant juice
½ dl (¼ cup) red wine vinegar
2 teaspoons salt
½ teaspoon ground cloves
½ teaspoon ground allspice
Sugar

Quarter the cabbage and remove the core. Shred as finely as possible. Peel and slice the onion. Peel, core and cut the apples into thin slices. Melt the butter in a heavy pot. Add the cabbage, onion and apple and sauté for a few minutes. Add remaining ingredients, cover and let simmer for around 40 minutes. Season with more salt, sugar and allspice, if necessary.

## ROOT VEGETABLE CARPACCIO
### ROTFRUKTSCARPACCIO

3 yellow beets
2 large carrots
2 parsnips
½ dl (¼ cup) chopped walnuts
½ dl (¼ cup) chopped hazelnuts
3 tablespoons olive oil
Coarse salt and freshly ground black pepper
2 tablespoons finely shredded flat-leaf parsley

Peel the vegetables and slice as thinly as possible. Blanch in salted water for around 2 minutes – they should be "al dente". Plunge into cold water. Arrange the vegetable slices in a single layer on a platter. Combine the nuts and sprinkle over the vegetables. Drizzle with oil and season with salt and pepper. Sprinkle with parsley.

## OPEN OMELET WITH SHELLFISH AND GRAVLAX
### ÖPPEN OMELETT MED SKALDJUR OCH GRAVLAX
(6 SERVINGS)

4 eggs
2 tablespoons milk
1 teaspoon salt
Freshly ground white pepper
½ dl (¼ cup) peeled shrimp
1 dl (½ cup) crayfish tails
½ dl (¼ cup) gravlax strips
1 tablespoon butter
1 tablespoon chopped parsley
1 tablespoon chopped dill

Crack the eggs into a bowl. Add milk, salt and pepper and beat until smooth. Combine the shellfish and salmon. Melt the butter in a hot skillet. Pour over the eggs, stirring lightly until they start to thicken. Even out the layer with a spatula. Turn out onto a platter and sprinkle with the seafood mixture and chopped herbs.

## OMELET WITH JERUSALEM ARTICHOKES, SPINACH AND PARMESAN

### OMELETT MED JORDÄRTSKOCKA, SPENAT OCH PARMESAN

(6 SERVINGS)

4 eggs
3 tablespoons milk
1 teaspoon salt
Freshly ground white pepper
200 g (7 ounces) Jerusalem artichokes
Butter
Olive oil
1 red onion
75 g (3 ounces) fresh spinach leaves
50 g (2 ounces) parmesan cheese

Crack the eggs into a bowl. Add milk, salt and pepper and beat until smooth. Peel and slice the Jerusalem artichokes. Fry in a little butter and olive oil. Peel and thinly slice the onion and add, frying until soft. Transfer to a plate and keep warm. Melt butter in the same pan and add the eggs, stirring lightly until they start to thicken. Spoon the artichoke-onion mixture onto half of the omelet. Fold over the other half. Arrange spinach on a serving tray. Place the omelet on the spinach. Cut the parmesan into thin flakes and sprinkle over the omelet.

## CRAYFISH-STYLE BALTIC HERRING
**KRÄFTSTRÖMMING**
(6 SERVINGS)

1 kg (2¼ pounds) fresh Baltic herring
1 tablespoon butter
1 tablespoon tomato paste
3 dl (1½ cups) tomato juice
1 dl (½ cup) beer
1 tablespoon dill seeds
1 tablespoon brown sugar
Salt and pepper

Preheat the oven to 175 C (350 F). Roll up the herring fillets, skin side out. Place in a greased ovenproof dish. Combine tomato paste, juice, beer and dill seeds in a saucepan and let simmer for 5 minutes. Stir in the brown sugar, salt and pepper. Pour over the fish and bake for around 15 minutes.

## CHRISTMAS MEATBALLS
**JULKÖTTBULLAR**
(6 SERVINGS)

1 large or 2 small onions
Butter
8 anchovy fillets
1 scant dl (⅓ cup) breadcrumbs
2 dl (¾ cup) milk
6 complete twists of the white pepper mill
1 teaspoon ground allspice
½ teaspoon ground cloves
300 g (10 ounces) ground pork
700 g (1½ pounds) ground beef
1 tablespoon salt
3 eggs
3 tablespoons corn syrup

Peel and mince the onion. Fry in butter until soft but not brown. Chop the anchovies and add, letting them "melt" into the onions. Let cool. Soak the breadcrumbs in the milk and add pepper, allspice and cloves. Mix the ground pork and beef with the salt. Add the eggs, onion mixture, breadcrumb-milk mixture and syrup, mixing well. Make a trial meatball and fry. Taste and correct seasoning, if necessary. Roll small meatballs and fry carefully, shaking the pan to brown evenly on all sides.

Make a large batch of these meatballs and freeze!

## PORK RIBS
**REVBENSSPJÄLL**
(6 SERVINGS

2 kg (4½ pounds) country style ribs or spareribs with the fresh bacon still on
2 tablespoons salt + 1 tablespoon white pepper
1 dl (½ cup) orange juice concentrate
1 tablespoon pickled ginger
1 tablespoon freshly grated ginger
2 twigs fresh rosemary
2 tablespoons sweet soy sauce (kecap manis)
2 pinches cayenne pepper
1 dl (½ cup) runny honey

Preheat the oven to 175 C (350 F). Rub the ribs with salt and pepper and place on a rack over a roasting pan, fat side up. Roast for 20 minutes. Combine the remaining ingredients, stirring well. Turn the ribs. Spoon the sauce over the ribs and roast for 20 minutes more. Turn and spoon more sauce over the meat. Roast for 20 minutes more. Turn one more time and lower the heat to 150 C (300 F). Roast for 20 minutes more. Check if the ribs are ready by either loosening a bone or poking with a skewer. If the juices are clear, the ribs are ready. Remove from the oven and let cool slightly. Cut into serving pieces along the bones.

## APPLESAUCE
**ÄPPLEMOS**
(6 SERVINGS)

1 kg (2¼ pounds) red apples, preferably small winter apples
3 tablespoons honey
1 dl (½ cup) brown sugar
1 twig fresh rosemary
2 teaspoons freshly grated ginger
3 tablespoons white wine vinegar

Quarter the apples, removing the cores. Cut into small dice. Place in a pot with the remaining ingredients. Heat to boiling, and let simmer for 15 minutes. Puree in a blender or food processor. Let cool and transfer to a lidded jar. Store in the refrigerator.

## LIVER PATÉ
**KALVLEVERPASTEJ**
(2 LOAVES)

800 g (1¾ pounds) calf's liver
280 g (10 ounces) fresh pork fat
1 onion
6 anchovy fillets with brine
1 tablespoon butter
4 tablespoons (¼ cup) Madeira
2 tablespoons cognac
5 eggs
1 dl (scant ½ cup) all-purpose flour
2 tablespoons potato starch
4 dl (1⅔ cups) whipping cream
2 teaspoons salt
1 teaspoon sodium nitrite (optional)
6 complete twists of the white pepper mill

Ask your butcher to grind the liver and pork fat into a medium coarse mixture. Preheat the oven to 175 C (350 F). Mince the onion and anchovies. Fry in butter until soft but not brown. Add the Madeira and cognac and let cool slightly. Beat together the eggs, flour, starch and cream. Stir in the ground liver and fat and the remaining ingredients, mixing well. Grease two loaf pans. Divide the liver mixture between the two pans. Bake for around 50 minutes. Test for doneness with a skewer. If it is almost dry, the patés are ready. Let cool completely. These patés can be cut into smaller pieces and frozen.

## PRESSED CUCUMBER SALAD
**PRESSGURKA**

1 large or 2 small seedless cucumbers
1 tablespoon salt
1 dl (½ cup) vinegar
2 dl (1 cup) sugar
3 dl (1½ cups) water
3 tablespoons chopped parsley

Peel the cucumber but leave a little of the green peel on for color. Slice as thinly as possible, preferably with a cheese plane and place in a bowl. Sprinkle with salt and refrigerate overnight. Place a weight over the cucumber slices (a dish with a can on top of it, for example) to press out as much liquid as possible. Whisk together vinegar, sugar and water. Drain the cucumber slices thoroughly, then add. Let marinate for at least 48 hours. Just before serving, sprinkle with parsley.

## NORTHERN DELIGHT
**SIKAFORSRÖRA**
(6 SERVINGS)

400 g (14 ounces) smoked reindeer (or beef), thinly sliced
4 cm (1½ inches) leek
1 dl (½ cup) mayonnaise
2 tablespoons grated fresh horseradish
3 tablespoons whitefish caviar
Crispbread

Cut the reindeer into thin strips. Shred the leek. Mix with the mayonnaise, horseradish and 1 tablespoon of the caviar. Form into small "eggs" and place on crispbread. Top with the remaining caviar.

## OLD MAN'S MIX
**LJUMMEN GUBBRÖRA**
(6 SERVINGS)

4 hard-cooked eggs
1 small onion
3 herring fillets
10 anchovy fillets
Butter
Freshly ground white pepper
2 tablespoons chopped chives
1 tablespoon caviar in a tube

Finely dice the eggs. Peel and mince the onion. Chop the herring and anchovies. Melt the butter and sauté eggs, onion, herring and anchovy lightly. Do not brown. Season with pepper and fold in chives and caviar. Serve on pumpernickel or other dark bread.

## LUTEFISK WITH PEAS, BECHAMEL SAUCE AND ALLSPICE

### LUTFISK MED GRÖNA ÄRTOR, VITSÅS OCH KRYDDPEPPAR

(6 SERVINGS)

600 g (1 ⅓ pounds) lutefisk
2 tablespoons butter
3 tablespoons all-purpose flour
5 ½ dl (2 ⅓ cups) milk
1 teaspoon salt
Pinch white pepper
1 teaspoon sugar

ACCOMPANIMENTS
Green peas
2 tablespoons butter
Salt and ground allspice
Boiled potatoes

Cut the lutefisk into 6 pieces of equal size and soak according to package directions. Cook carefully in lightly salted water to cover for around 20 minutes. Test with a skewer. If it penetrates the fish with no resistance, the fish is ready.

Melt the butter and whisk in the flour. Lower the heat and whisk in half the milk. Heat to boiling, stirring constantly. Add the remaining milk and let simmer for 5 minutes, stirring occasionally. Do not allow the sauce to burn. Season with salt, white pepper and sugar.

Heat the peas in butter. Season with salt. Serve the fish with the sauce, peas, allspice and boiled potatoes. Coarsely ground mustard is good with this dish.

## SWEET WORT BREAD
**VÖRTBRÖD**
(4 LOAVES)

100 g (3½ ounces) butter
6 dl (2½ cups) dark beer
4 dl (1½ cups) low alcohol beer
50 g (1¾ ounces) fresh yeast
1½ dl (⅔ cup) dark corn syrup
1 tablespoon salt
2 teaspoons ground cloves
2 tablespoons ground bitter orange peel
3 dl (1¼ cups) raisins
3 liters (12½ cups) sifted rye flour
1–2 dl (½–¾ cups) all-purpose flour

Melt the butter and add the two beers. Heat to lukewarm. Crumble the yeast into the liquid. Add syrup, salt, spices and raisins. Add the rye flour and knead well. Cover and let rise for one hour. Knead with all-purpose flour and divide into 4 pieces of equal size. Form into loaves. Place on an oven tray or in greased bread pans. Cover and let rise for 30 minutes. Preheat the oven to 200 C (400 F). Bake for 35 minutes. These loaves freeze well.

## CHEESE PLATTER
**OSTFAT**

*Cheeses for the Christmas table:*
Spiced cheese from Småland
Cheddar
Västerbottenost (full-flavored hard cheese)
Stilton

Red Edam cheese is synonymous with Christmas for most people, but the cheeses listed above have much more character and complement the rich foods of Christmas much better.

## GINGERBREAD LOAF
**MJUK PEPPARKAKA**

100 g (3½ ounces) butter, softened
2 dl (scant 1 cup) brown sugar
2 eggs
1½ dl (⅔ cup) buttermilk or natural yogurt (3% fat)
3 dl (1¼ cups) all-purpose flour
1 tablespoon ground cinnamon
1 teaspoon ground cloves
1 teaspoon ground ginger
1 teaspoon baking soda
½ dl (3½ tablespoons) dark corn syrup
2 tablespoons lingonberry preserves

Preheat the oven to 160 C (325 F). Grease and flour a loaf pan. Beat the butter and sugar until light and fluffy. Add the eggs. Beat in the buttermilk/yogurt. Combine flour, spices and baking soda and fold into the egg mixture. Stir in the syrup and preserves. Pour into the prepared pan. Bake for 55 minutes.

## RICE PORRIDGE
**RISGRYNSGRÖT**
(6 SERVINGS)

4 dl (1 2/3 cups) short grain rice
8 dl (3 1/3 cups) water
2 teaspoons salt
3 tablespoons butter
2 cinnamon sticks
1½ liters (6 1/3 cups) milk
2 tablespoons sugar

In a heavy pot, heat rice, water, salt and butter to boiling. Lower heat and cook for 10 minutes. Add cinnamon sticks and half the milk. Reheat to boiling, stirring constantly. Lower heat and let simmer slowly for 10 minutes, adding the remaining milk as it cooks. Do not allow to boil. Remove from the heat and let the porridge "swell" for 20 minutes. Stir in sugar and more salt, if needed. Serve with cinnamon and sugar or blueberry jam. Don't forget the almonds!

## SAFFRON PANCAKE
**SAFFRANSPANNKAKA**
(6 SERVINGS)

1 teaspoon saffron threads
2 dl (1 cup) whipping cream
1 ½ dl (¾ cup) milk
3 eggs
2 tablespoons chopped almonds
5 dl (2 cups) rice porridge
*(see previous recipe)*

Preheat the oven to 175 C (350 F). Dissolve the saffron in the cream and milk. Beat the eggs and almonds and fold into the porridge. Pour into a greased ovenproof dish. Bake for around 30 minutes, until set. Serve as is or with blueberry-raspberry preserves.

## RICE À LA MALTA
**RIS À LA MALTA**
(6 SERVINGS)

6 dl (2½ cups) rice porridge
*(see recipe same page)*
3 dl (1¼ cups) whipping cream
2 tablespoons sugar
2 teaspoons vanilla sugar
or 1 teaspoon vanilla extract
2 oranges

The rice porridge should be very cold. Whip the cream with the sugar and vanilla sugar. Fold into the porridge. Transfer to a serving bowl. Peel the oranges and separate into sections, removing all the membrane. Arrange in a pinwheel pattern on top of the rice cream.

### DEEP-FRIED COOKIES WITH WARM CLOUDBERRIES AND WHIPPED CREAM
**KLENÄTER MED VARMA HJORTRON OCH VISPGRÄDDE**
(6 SERVINGS

4 egg yolks
3½ tablespoons sugar
Pinch salt
Grated zest of one lemon
2 tablespoons unsalted butter
2 tablespoons vodka
3 dl (1¼ cups) all-purpose flour
7½ dl (3 cups) corn or safflower oil for frying

GARNISH
3½ tablespoons sugar
2 tablespoons cinnamon
2 dl (1 cup) cloudberry preserves or compote
2 dl (1 cup) whipping cream

Beat egg yolks, sugar, salt and lemon zest until light and lemon-colored. Melt the butter with the vodka. Let cool slightly and add to the egg yolk mixture. Add the flour, mixing well. The dough should be smooth. Cover and refrigerate overnight.

Roll out the dough into 3 mm thick sheets. Using a ruler and a pastry wheel, cut 3 cm (1¼ inch) wide and 12 cm (5 inch) long strips of dough. Cut a lengthwise slit in the center of each and pull one end of the strip through the slit, so that the long sides are twisted. Heat the oil in a heavy pot that holds at least 2 liters/quarts. Be sure to have a lid within reach. Heat to 180 C (350 F). The oil should be lightly smoking . Using a slotted spoon, place the cookies in the oil, about 10 at a time. Fry for one minute. Transfer to paper towels to drain. Combine sugar and cinnamon and dip the cookies into the mixture. Serve with cloudberry preserves and whipped cream.

### BURNT ALMONDS
**BRÄNDA MANDLAR**

We recommend that you buy burnt almonds instead of making them. Those available at Christmas markets are excellent, and then you can do other things with your time.

### SAFFRON BISCOTTI
**SAFFRANSBISCOTTI**
(AROUND 40 BISCOTTI)

200 g (7 ounces) butter
2 teaspoons saffron threads
3 dl (1¼ cups) sugar
1 liter (4¼ cups) all-purpose flour
2 teaspoons vanilla sugar or 1 teaspoon vanilla extract
1 tablespoon baking powder
1 dl (½ cup) chopped almonds
1 dl (½ cup) chopped hazelnuts
4 eggs

Preheat the oven to 175 C (350 F). Melt the butter and add the saffron. Combine the dry ingredients and mix in the saffron butter. Add the eggs and mix well. Knead the dough until smooth. Divide into 4 pieces of equal size and roll into lengths. Place onto parchment-lined baking sheet and bake until golden, around 15 minutes. Remove from the oven and cut into 1 cm (½ inch) slices. Reduce the oven temperature to 100 C (210 F) and let the slices "dry" in the oven for around 1 hour. Store in an air-tight tin.

### ICE CHOCOLATE
**ISCHOKLAD**
(AROUND 50)

250 g (9 ounces) good quality semi-sweet chocolate
200 g (7 ounces) coconut fat
4 tablespoons raisins
2 tablespoons dark rum or cognac
50 small foil candy cups

Break the chocolate and coconut fat into small chunks and melt over very low heat. Stir until blended. Chop the raisins and add with the rum or cognac. Spoon into individual foil cups and let cool. Store in an air-tight tin in the refrigerator.

### CARAMELS
**KNÄCK**
(AROUND 70)

3 dl (1 cup) whipping cream
3 dl (1 cup) corn syrup
3 dl (1 cup) sugar
1 dl (⅓ cup) chopped almonds
70 small paper candy cups

Place the cream, syrup and sugar in a pot and boil for 15 minutes. If you have a candy thermometer, it should read 122 C (218 F). Stir in the almonds. Spoon into individual paper cups and let cool. Store in an air-tight tin.

### MINT KISSES
**MINTKYSSAR**
(AROUND 60)

4 dl (2 cups) powdered sugar
1 dl (½ cup) water
1 tablespoon vinegar
10 drops peppermint oil
50 g (2 ounces) good quality semi-sweet or bittersweet chocolate

Combine sugar, water and vinegar in a heavy pot and simmer for around 10 minutes. Check the consistency by wetting two fingers in cold water, then take a drop of the mixture between the fingers and pull them apart. If it forms a thread, it is ready.

Pour the mixture into an oiled bowl. When cooled but not yet cold, add the peppermint oil and mix well with a fork. Place the bowl over a saucepan of boiling water and stir until the mixture thickens.

Place spoonfuls of the mixture on parchment paper and let set. Melt the chocolate and drop small spoonfuls onto the mints. Store in a box or tin with parchment between each layer so they don't stick together.

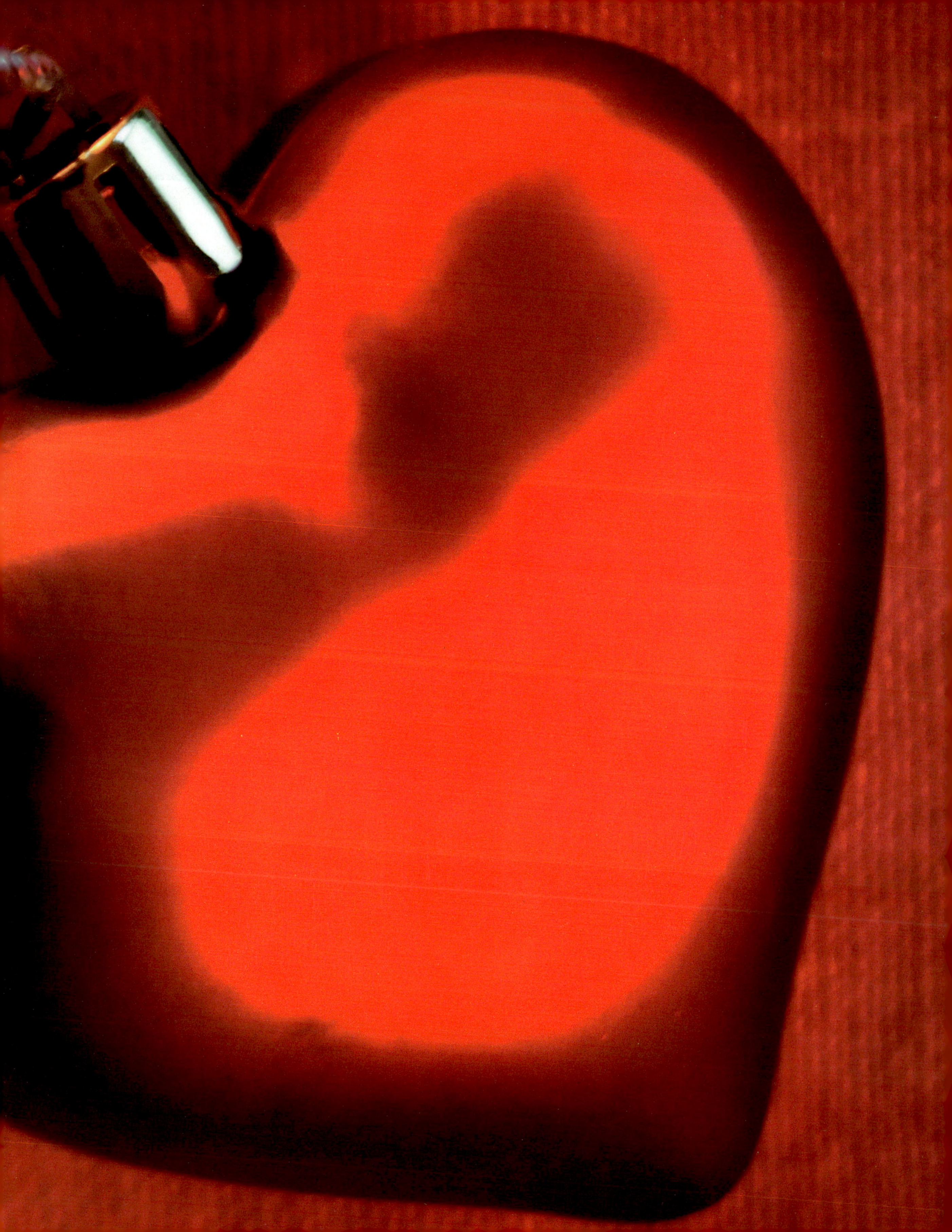

## FRESH FRUIT SALAD
### FÄRSK FRUKTSALLAD
(6 SERVINGS)

½ honeydew melon
2 blue plums
3 kiwi fruits
1 pineapple
2 oranges
3 passion fruits
1 liter (quart) strawberries
1 bunch seedless grapes

Peel the melon and remove the seeds. Peel the plums and kiwi fruits. Peel and core the pineapple. Cut into bite-size pieces. Juice the oranges. Halve the passion fruit and scoop out the fruit. Combine with the remaining ingredients. Serve as is or with softened vanilla ice cream.

## GRANDFATHER'S GLÖGG

*(strong and warming)*

**FARFARS GLÖGG**

(6 SERVINGS)

1 bitter orange peel
2 teaspoons grated fresh ginger
3 cinnamon sticks
10 cloves
3 star anise
10 cardamom seeds
1 dl (½ cup) water
1½ dl (¾ cup) sugar
1 dl (½ cup) dark rum (inexpensive)
2 dl (1 cup) cognac (inexpensive)
7½ dl (3¾ cups) red wine

Heat spices and water to boiling. Remove from the heat and let steep overnight. Strain and remove spices. Combine the spiced liquid with the remaining ingredients and heat slowly. Do not allow to boil. Serve with blanched almonds, raisins and gingerbread cookies.

## MY BROTHER'S DRINK

**MIN BRORS MUMMA**

(3 SERVINGS)

½ bottle ginger ale
1 bottle dark beer
1 bottle beer
3–4 tablespoons gin.

Combine all ingredients and serve from a decorative carafe.

## MANNERHEIM'S SCHNAPPS

**MANNERHEIMS SNAPS**

(3 SERVINGS)

*"Christmas without the marshall's schnapps is like Christmas without Santa Claus"*

5 dl (2 cups) vodka
5 dl (2 cups) Skåne aquavit
2 teaspoons gin
4 teaspoons dry vermouth

Combine all ingredients and serve well chilled.

OMELET WITH JERUSALEM ARTICHOKES, SPINACH AND PARMESAN .......... 40

PROFESSOR LALLERSTEDT'S MUSTARD-MARINATED SMOKED HERRING .........21

PORK RIBS ..................47

RICE À LA MALTA ..........56

ROOT VEGETABLE CARPACCIO ........................................ 39

SAFFRON PANCAKE ...................................................... 56

MUSTARD HERRING......18

NORTHERN DELIGHT ... 51

HERRING SALAD.......... 23

SWEET WORT BREAD ........................55

EGG HALVES WITH SHRIMP, ANCHOVIES AND MAYONNAISE ........32

OPEN OMELET WITH SHELLFISH AND GRAVLAX.................39

**THE CHRISTMAS TABLE'S ABC**

**THE FIRST ROUND AT THE CHRISTMAS TABLE:**



**THE SECOND ROUND AT THE CHRISTMAS TABLE:**



**THE THIRD ROUND AT THE CHRISTMAS TABLE:**

## THE FOURTH ROUND AT THE CHRISTMAS TABLE:



## THE FIFTH ROUND AT THE CHRISTMAS TABLE:



## CHRISTMAS TABLE DRINKS:



## CHRISTMAS TABLE BREAD AND BAKED GOODS:

NOTE FOR THE ENGLISH EDITION:
When preparing the recipes, follow the measurements either in metric or imperial; deciliters or cups (1 cup = 8 fluid ounces = 2½ dl). Do not combine the two systems within one recipe.

THANKS TO:
ENEBYBERGS ANTIK
MATEUS STOCK
AGNETA LIVIJN

WWW.ICABOKFORLAG.SE



FORMA PUBLISHING GROUP AB IS MILIEU-CERTIFIED ACCORDING TO ISO 14001

ENGLISH TRANSLATION: MELODY FAVISH

RECIPES: ERIK LALLERSTEDT OCH MAGNUS LEIDSTEDT
PHOTOS: BRUNO EHRS
PHOTO ASSISTENT: TOMAS TELIN
PROJECT LEADER, REKVISITA: INGELA HOLM
EDITOR: GUNILLA WAGNER
ART DIRECTOR: PELLE SUNDQUIST
CREATIVE CONSULTANT: PELLE HOLM
ORIGINAL: PELLE SUNDQUIST
REPRO: DONE
PRINTED: IGF, ITALIEN 2008

ISBN 978-91-534-3124-4